Keepsakes or Mistakes: *Why Some Things Should Never Be Kept,* by Dr. Marlene Miles

Freshwater Press 2025

Freshwaterpress9@gmail.com

ISBN: 978-1-967860-31-9

Paperback Version

Table of Contents

Prologue 5

Introduction 8

Origin Matters: The Spirit Behind the Gift 15

Prayer of Release & Cleansing 18

The Fraternity Funeral 20

Rachel Took the Idols 23

Objects Carrying Spiritual Weight in the Bible 29

Fighting for What Will Harm You? 32

Beauty Items 39

What's Inherited 45

The Breakup, The Soul Tie 56

Prayer for Breaking Unhealthy Soul Ties 58

What's In a Name? 60

Infertility & Worse Problems 65

Teraphim, Terrapin--- DELAYS! 72

Your Father's House 76

Your Daddy's Suit: Garments 79

Souvenirs 84

Rachel Died 95

Can't Get Rid of Some Things (Easily). 103

Return to Me 107

When Did You First Notice? 110

PRAYERS 116

Dear Reader 124

Prayerbooks by this author 125

Other books by this author 127

KEEPSAKES or MISTAKES

Why Some Things Should Never Be Kept

Freshwater

Prologue

Some things hold memories. Others hold bondage.

We've all kept things for sentimental reasons — a gift, a token, a keepsake. But what if that harmless object isn't harmless at all? What if it carries spiritual baggage, you never saw coming?

Keepsakes or Mistakes: ***Why Some Things Should Never Be Kept*** is a wake-up call to examine what you've allowed into your life, your home, and your heart.

From inherited items to innocent souvenirs, this book will show you how the enemy hides in plain sight — and how you can break free from the unseen burdens you've been carrying.

It's   not   superstition. It's spiritual survival.

I *am* the LORD: that *is* my name: and
my glory will I not give to another,
neither my praise to graven images.
(Isaiah 42:8)

Introduction

Greetings, saints of God. I want to share something today that could be the answer to your problem or problems. This could be a book for deep deliverance for you. It could be life changing, or you could gloss over it and miss the entire thing. It's your choice.

Keepsakes, things you inherit from grandma, grandpa. Is everything you inherit, every gift you receive a good thing to keep? If you are a sentimental person, or have a *hoarding spirit* you may have trouble getting rid of things that are in your possession that may not be good for you to have.

When you take things or accept things from people – it could look like décor, art, or jewelry to you, watches. but it may be a whole idol to them, whether they realized it or not. Inherited items are usually things that the benefactor or gift giver has held onto for a while. It could be their "prize possession."

This thing that they've kept precious for so long may not have caused them a moment's harm and no spiritual danger, but then again, it may have and they may have been oblivious to it. It depends on that person and what their spiritual life was about or like. If they were a non-Christian, a slack Christian or something worse, such as a person in the dark kingdom, whether you realized it or not, this item could have been for them, or it may become for the next person who has it a point of contact to the dark kingdom. It may have a satanic or occultic leaning to them. There may be a satanic or occult charge or history on the item, and without discernment from the Holy Spirit, you may not know anything about that.

For example, it is estimated that there are about 6 million people practicing Freemasonry worldwide with most of them in the United States. But their society is a secret. In the US we see numbers in the low millions, but only in the low 100 thousands in other countries of the world. The numbers have declined over the decades — especially in the U.S. and U.K. — mostly due to aging membership and less public interest. While the group is known for secrecy, the existence of lodges and national membership figures is openly reported by many Grand Lodges.

Other secret societies may include:

- Odd Fellows
- Rosicrucian
- Skull & Bones-type college societies
- Ancient Orders (like the Druids)
- Secret political or activist cells
- Some religious or occult societies
- Shriners

The Shriners (originally the Ancient Arabic Order of the Nobles of the Mystic Shrine) are a branch of Freemasonry founded in 1870. To become a Shriner, you must first be a Master Mason — so it's an extension of the Masonic system. They are known for hospitals, parades, and charitable works — but their imagery and rituals have deeper meanings.

`Why the Concern Spiritually?** Their symbols and regalia include **Islamic and occultic imagery** (e.g., scimitars, crescents, sphinxes). Their initiation rites historically involved oaths invoking **Arabic deities or phrases** not aligned with biblical truth. Like Masonry, they operate with **secrecy, ritual, and symbolic allegiances** — elements commonly associated with occult practice.

The Deceptive Blend is because Shriners mix **public charity with private secrecy** — which makes them seem harmless or even noble. They advertise on tv, right in your face and ask you to give them money. What happens when you give to an occultic altar? What happens when you receive from an occultic altar? You get initiated. You owe them. What parent wouldn't say yes to someone paying for their unwell child's hospitalization.

But spiritual allegiance doesn't change because someone does good works. The underlying system is still rooted in secret oaths and unscriptural alliances.

What fellowship has light with darkness?
(2 Corinthians 6:14-17)

Have nothing to do with the fruitless deeds
of darkness, but rather expose them.
(Ephesians 5:11)

The point is that secret societies are most often occultic and they have paraphernalia, items that they use in the practice of their craft. Those items don't all stay at the lodge, the shrine, or the coven, but they flood out into the regular world, and they can be dangerous to even innocent people who don't believe in any of this.

Sadly, these figures regarding secret societies don't include hate groups such as: The Ku Klux Klan (KKK) is typically classified as a **hate group** and **domestic terrorist organization**, not a secret society in the fraternal or traditional sense.

However, the KKK shares some features with secret societies:

- Initiation rituals
- Hierarchical ranks and titles

- Use of symbolism, robes, and secret codes
- Oath-bound secrecy
- Local "chapters" called klaverns

But its core identity is rooted in racist ideology, violence, and political intimidation, so most scholars group the KKK under:

- Extremist political organizations

- White supremacist hate groups

- Domestic terrorist networks

It's distinct from traditional secret societies like Freemasons or collegiate groups, whose aims are social, fraternal, or esoteric rather than violent or political.

While it operates *like* a secret society in structure, it's generally classified as an extremist political movement.

So, if you got grandpa's KKK hood, would you keep it just because it's grandpa's?

In the U.S.: The Southern Poverty Law Center (SPLC) tracks about 700–800 active hate groups, with tens of thousands of members. In Europe, far-right and neo-Nazi groups are active in Germany, France, Eastern Europe — also in the tens of thousands. In Russia: Nationalist hate groups have been strong, though often linked to political movements.

In Latin America, Africa, Asia: Hate groups exist but tend to blend with militias, gangs, or political extremist cells.

Certainly, your relative was never involved in any of this, so there is no chance that they could ever have possessed anything spiritually harmful or brought any such thing into the house you grew up in, or left any such thing to you---, *right*?

Origin Matters: The Spirit Behind the Gift

Objects can carry **spiritual significance** based on who gave them or where they came from. In some belief systems, gifts can be "charged" with intentions — good *or* harmful. For example, jewelry or items linked to toxic exes, occult practices, or even stolen goods.

Some traditions teach that objects can carry **attachments** — spirits, curses, or lingering negative energy. Things used in rituals, secret societies, occult practices, or even dark family histories may bring unseen problems into a person's life.

Unknowingly receiving something innocently doesn't mean it's spiritually harmless. Neither does declaring you don't believe in witchcraft protect you from anything --, and especially witchcraft. Witches love people who don't believe they exist or have power; that is what keeps their acts occultic, or hidden. Wearing a charm from a tourist market that was actually crafted for witchcraft or sold with malicious intent.

A curse without cause will not alight.
Proverbs 26:2

But opening your life to unknown things may invite trouble.

Some believe gifts create **soul ties** — emotional, spiritual links — especially if given in manipulation, lust, or deceit. In that case, the gift becomes a "tether" back to that person or situation.

In Acts 19:19 believers burned sorcery scrolls publicly when they came to Christ. In Joshua 7 — Achan kept forbidden things, and it cursed the whole camp.

Don't assume every "harmless" keepsake is neutral. Therefore, It is wise to pray over and discern items you receive. You don't have to live paranoid — but live aware.

Sometimes, letting go of certain items brings freedom, peace, and spiritual clarity.

Prayer of Release & Cleansing

Father God, in the name of Jesus,

I come before You with an open
heart and a willing spirit.
I thank You for Your truth that sets me free.
I ask You now — search my heart, search
my home, search my life.

If there are any objects, gifts,
keepsakes, or possessions in my life
that carry darkness, manipulation, control,
or ungodly influence, reveal them to me by
Your Spirit.

I renounce every tie, every curse,
every hidden work of the enemy
that has tried to enter my life through these
things.
I break agreement with anything not of You.

I release it, I let it go, and I close every door to the enemy,
by the blood of Jesus Christ.

Father, cleanse my space. Cleanse my heart.
Fill every room with Your presence.
Let my home be a dwelling place for Your Spirit alone.

Thank You for freedom.
Thank You for peace.
Thank You for wisdom.

In Jesus' Name. Amen.

The Fraternity Funeral

Modern secret societies show up in colleges, culture, and beyond. While most people think of secret societies in terms of Freemasonry or the Eastern Star, the spirit of secrecy, ritual, and hidden allegiance shows up in more places than we realize — including college campuses.

Many Greek-letter fraternities and sororities, particularly those founded in the 18th and 19th centuries, were shaped by Masonic ideals. Their founders were often Freemasons, and their organizations mirror the structure of Masonic lodges — with oaths, rituals, degrees, secret handshakes, and symbolic language. For many young people, these college organizations are the first exposure to a culture of secrecy, spiritual vows, and brotherhoods that operate outside the light of God's truth.

Although not every member progresses into Freemasonry or Eastern Star, the overlap is undeniable. In some cultural spaces, especially among historically Black fraternities and sororities, Masonic ties are even stronger. What starts as tradition or status can become spiritual entanglement — particularly if one has made vows or taken oaths that spiritually bind them without discernment.

Fraternity and sorority logos paraphernalia and gear usually bear the images of idols and college kids can carry these for a lifetime even renewing their allegiances yearly. These idols can consume a life even unto death.

One frat bro even took his idols into the afterlife; he had a fraternity funeral as if those idols had a heaven to put him in. how deceived he was. How entangled. Won't he be surprised to find that all of his devotion to his idols even though they may have given him what he wanted in this life only had steps that led straight to hell in the afterlife. He may have gotten acceptance and favor from other frat bro's, recognition and even a leg up in business, but there is no Heaven attached to any idol. There is not eternal life, salvation or redemption.

Rachel Took the Idols

Rachel took her father's idols, teraphim...a graven image, revering to an image that is an idol. and refused to give them back.

Rachel, the daughter of Laban in the biblical narrative, takes her father's household idols when she leaves with Jacob who had finally left Laban's ranch. He took with him Leah, their children, concubines, and their children and also Rachel who had not had any children yet. He took all that cattle. Rachel took Laban's idols with her.

Curiosity makes me want to know what happened to the idols:

Rachel steals the idols as they symbolize her father's household *gods* that he worshipped. In Rachel's mind they could have possibly been her claim to her inheritance. We know Laban changed Jacob's wages and terms of their agreement more than once. The Scripture also says that he had taken all from Leah and from Rachel. Perhaps she took the idols for monetary reasons.

When Laban came running after them-- not to get his kids back or his grandkids--, no Laban pursues Jacob to recover the idols. Laban searches through all their belongings like a TSA Agent, but Rachel wouldn't get up off her camel. In the saddle is where she had hidden the idols. She said it was her time of the month, and she couldn't get off the camel. So, Laban did not find or recover the idols.

But isn't that just like idols? They get in a bloodline, and they pass from one generation to the next. The idols have no inherent power to jump into the camel's saddle or anyplace else, but we humans pick these things up and move them from place to place and from person to person. While having an item that is an idol may not make a person an idolater; it can make them idolatry-adjacent.

Rachel hides the idols by placing them in her camel's saddle and sitting on them, claiming she cannot rise due to it being her time of the month. Don't miss the irony here as demons, devils, and strongmen are often said to "sit on a person's life," to hold them back from progress.

This tells us a lot about Rachel and her relationship with her father. The idols represent something about Rachel. Did she take the idols to irritate her father? Did she take the idols because she knew what they were and wanted them to protect her?

To me: the story shows dissension in a marriage where one is serving the Only Living God and his new wife, the one he loves so much, the other of the couple is a hypocrite, possibly serving more than one God – hedging bets. This story starts around Genesis 31:19-35. Maybe Rachel was clueless --, maybe she was serving no god. Maybe she was just pretending.

A 50-year-old man who is a pastor married his wife when he was young, so they've been married a couple of decades now. she doesn't believe in God; and he is clueless about that fact to this very day. When a man, or a woman marries another for shallow or flesh reasons, that spouse is called a trophy. Usually, the other doesn't care about their beliefs, their interests, their mind, or their spiritual life. He just wants a marriage, and he wants her to look, or be a certain way or have a certain amount of wealth. Usually. That pastor has been married to his wife for about 30 years.

In 21 years of Jacob being on Laban's ranch he seemed to know little about Rachel. And as we read the Bible, we know a couple of things: she was prettier than Leah. She was younger than Leah. She was at least a thief, and at most an idolater.

But maybe she just did what she was told as women during that time did. They did what they had to do to get along.

Rachel then had issues with infertility.

Rachel had difficulty in childbirth – more so with Benjamin than Joseph --- Joseph had problems--, problems that we usually blame Joseph for causing because of his big mouth. But Joseph's big mouth didn't get him thrown in jail from Potiphar's house, did it? Actually, Joseph's mouth is what got him OUT of jail, so it was more of who Joseph told things to than what he told them. (Possibly).

Remember, Rachel died right after giving birth to Benoni, the child of her pain.

Rachel took the idols; Rachel had the idols. Rachel even lied to her father and wouldn't give them back.

Sometimes idols are gifts, sometimes these gifts are intentional. Sometimes these idols are coveted, and people pursue them--, didn't Laban? Didn't Rachel? Sometimes people know these are idols, accursed or demonically charged things and they may try to acquire them for nefarious reasons. But, sometimes these keepsakes, trinkets or other items just fall into your hands.

A woman said that ever since she received her aunt's ring after her aunt passed on, that woman's back has been hurting. Severely. A point of contact for demons. Idols are demons, idols are devils, idols are little g *gods*.

Objects Carrying Spiritual Weight in the Bible

In Joshua 7 (Achan's Sin): The "accursed thing" didn't just affect Achan — it brought defeat on Israel.

In Acts 19:19 (Ephesus): Believers publicly burned their occult objects — even though they were costly.

In Exodus 32 (Golden Calf): Objects of worship became snares, even when people thought it was "just a symbol."

When keepsakes are tied to sin, trauma, or bondage they carry a spiritual burden. Items linked to sexual sin, witchcraft, blood oaths, or manipulation are of special concern.

- Letters, photos, jewelry, clothing — all can hold emotional and spiritual influence if connected to sin.

Cultural artifacts can bring spiritual baggage. Idols or "decor" from certain cultures may have been created for worship or sorcery — even if sold as souvenirs.

. Educate yourself before bringing things into your home. W*isdom is the principal thing* (Proverbs 4:7)

The Enemy uses innocence and ignorance to lure and trap souls. Satan loves hidden doorways — if he can't attack front-on, he'll use subtle, symbolic things. Not every attack is random — sometimes it's tied to what we keep close.

My people perish for lack of knowledge.
(Hosea 4:6)

Practical steps for Believers include praying over gifts before accepting or keeping them. If you feel unsettled, don't ignore it, you may step into a world of hurt. The Holy Spirit is in our life to warn us of dangers. Don't fear — but be willing to release anything the Lord tells you to.

Fighting for What Will Harm You?

Fighting over jewelry and other keepsakes from grandma or whomever- can often happen in families when wills are read and inheritances are doled out. Some will fight like a prophetic vulture before the person even dies. But let's say there was a squabble over a certain item and maybe you won.

Yay?

You got the item and your sibling or other relative did not. But did you really win?

What does your life look like since you got that item? Since you got that cameo, that broach, or those earrings, or that painting that you loved so much and put on the wall?

Now that your loved one has gone on to glory and you have acquired this old -- thing? How's your life?

God says, **"Behold, I do a new thing."**

There is nothing wrong with old things. I used to love old things, thinking they were unique, peculiar--, cool. Of course, the sales campaign is that those things were better made back then, the quality is so much better. Much of that can be very true, but does it make it expedient to own that item, or have it in your home or office? They don't make them like this anymore, but it is not as much about how it was made or the quality of its creation or manufacturing. It is more about who had possession of it. Whose life was this item in? What life or *spirit* was put into this item by virtue of ownership, handling, or intention? You should know that because this is more than a footrace baton that just got handed to you, where you'll run a lap around the track and then quickly hand it off to someone else.

And, it's not about time; handling it for a few minutes versus handling it for an hour may not matter, depending on how the item has been charged and what is your spiritual awareness and covering to protect you from *enchanted* items?

Two things can look identical, one can become an idol and the other is not. A child's toy--, an action figure, might it not look like an idol or figurine—such as Pokemon? Without discernment how will we know? Do we wait for it to start talking or for our child to manifest in its presence?

Whatever you get, old or new, whatever style – be sure to pray over it consecrate it, dedicate it to the Lord for proper use. Then listen to the Holy Spirit to be sure that what you are getting or bringing into your home, or your life <u>CAN</u> be dedicated and that it CAN be consecrated to the Lord. Listen closely to be sure that the thing you want to consecrate to the Lord CAN be consecrated.

It's not like God is not more powerful than anything or anyone, but some things are

beyond redemption. Like what? Oh, I don't know—food dedicated to idols. Masks and items used in rituals. How are you going to bless spirit food? It is said that it is human flesh and human blood, so how do you dedicate those things to God? How do you bless those things?

The devil and his fallen angels cannot be redeemed. So, anything of theirs or anything that represents them cannot be "blessed" even by a Christian.

Items used in rituals. There is a man who has masks hung on the walls of his house. He thinks it makes his house look all man-*cavey*---, People have told him for some time to take them down, saying those masks have been used in ritual. And perhaps they have.

It's *very possible* — depending on where the mask came from and its design.

The chances that an African mask of a goat has been used in ritual ceremonies may be very high. In many African cultures, the **goat** is symbolically tied to sacrifice, ancestral offerings, or spiritual rituals. Masks shaped like goat heads (or antelope, ram) are often used in ritual dances, ancestral ceremonies, or initiation rites — sometimes for good, sometimes for control or occult practice.

- Some masks represent fertility, harvest, or spirits of the dead. Others are used in secret society rituals (e.g., Poro, Egungun, or Nyamwezi groups).

If the Mask Came From: West Africa (Mali, Nigeria, Ivory Coast, many of the masks from those areas are tied to spiritual societies.

- **Central Africa (Congo regions):** Masks are often linked to ancestral worship or spiritual intermediaries.

- **Tourist Shops:** Some are mass-produced, but others are *real*, resold without disclosure.

What raises concern is:

- Carved in traditional style with ritual patterns

- Described as "authentic" or "tribal" from a known secret society region

- Signs of wear that suggest it was *used*, not just decorative

The bottom line is, if you saw a goat-head mask from Africa, there's a high chance it was either Made for or inspired by ritual purposes. Or, possibly used in a ceremony — especially if handcrafted and not a souvenir knockoff

And if your spirit checked you about it, trust your spirit, especially if you have the Holy Spirit.

The spiritual significance behind those items is not superstition — it's reality in many traditional African practices.

Not every culture's art is benign and spiritually neutral. Some artifacts represent ancestral worship, idol crafts, or occult symbols. Objects may carry spiritual baggage. Just because it's pretty or handmade doesn't mean it's harmless. **Your** home is your sanctuary. What you bring in affects the atmosphere of your space. God's people are called to discern, not collect. It is the world teaches us to gather trinkets. The Word teaches us to guard our gates.

Ask these questions before bringing something home:

- Do I know what this object represents in its original culture?

- Is there any spiritual history attached to this type of artifact?

- Does this honor God, or could it conflict with my faith?

- Am I buying this because it's beautiful — or because it's meaningful?

Everything you admire isn't meant for you to acquire.

It's okay to bring home mementos, but make sure they're clean spiritually. When in doubt, leave it. Your peace is worth more than a souvenir.

Beauty Items

Human hair gotten off a cadaver, processed and repackaged in bundles for extensions? How are you going to bless that? I don't think a bundle can just fall into your possession, but stranger things have happened.

Many years ago, it was suggested that I get my hair braided. I did – it took hours and hours. An old woman that I thought was my friend then, but have come to know she is a witch, yes, a whole witch— who happened to have made the suggestion, sat there the entire 6 hours with me.

Why?

I used to think it was so I either wouldn't talk about her to the hair stylist, or that the stylist wouldn't tell me anything about this woman. Then I thought perhaps it was to get a cut of the money that I paid the stylist to do the braiding.

Could have been.

But many years have passed and I now, in retrospect, see she was a witch, so maybe she was there for all those reasons and maybe she was there for some of my hair.

Why?

For bewitchment.

This witch worked across the hall in the first professional office that was all mine. While in those long, beautiful braids, many things that I didn't think would ever happen to me happened to me. I remember a car accident in particular. Nothing was broken but I had chronic pain, needed meds, and lost momentum and a great deal of time from work.

That is the office where I was working when I had the debilitating car accident. Yet, a week before that accident a car that was traveling beside me drifted suddenly into my lane, then it sped off like a crazy or drunk driver. That was the day Jesus took the wheel and my car even though I was driving it, it was as though the steering wheel started moving by itself to get me further over to the right to keep that speeding car from sideswiping me.

Praise be to God. Thank You, Jesus!

No thanks to the witch but in those days, people being witches was not on my radar. Of note, there was no one chasing this speeding driver and no one in front of this driver and it was a one-way street with two lanes, plenty of room for him to simply drive and there was no one in front of him impeding his passage. He never was behind me, so he wasn't frustrated with me keeping the speed limit; he was always in the other lane until he sped into my lane.

That was a week before another old lady driver with the giant car T-boned my beautiful new car.

Was this the work of the woman who now had some of my hair? Take your guesses. I also recall now that everything I told her that I liked or desired for my life would suddenly dry up.

There was a fellow that I had been friends with for years and wanted to date him seriously. He came to my office at least once a week just to say hello, just to visit. Then one day, poof, he stopped coming to see me and he stopped calling me.

Before him, there was another fellow that I desperately wanted to break up with but one day when I got back to work after a needed vacation he was in my office. The office wasn't open, but he was in it. How did he get in? she had a key, but that thought didn't occur to me. I thought that he had picked the lock.

Was he there to apologize to me, beg me to come back to him, or to threaten me? He had a Bible in his arms as if he had found the Lord. I didn't believe that for a moment, but especially when I saw he had cut the Bible out like an outlaw might do in an old Western movie to hide a gun. He didn't have a gun, but inside that cut out was a scalpel with a blade in it. It all had fallen to the floor when he opened the Bible. .

Quickly I Reached down and grabbed the scalpel, exclaiming, *That's mine! How did you get that?* I held it as a weapon, since it was mine after all, and I was not afraid of it—or him. In anger and instinctively I slashed the air with it in his direction.

He hauled it out of there leaving the cut-out Bible and he never came back to my place of business or my house again.

Excitedly, I ran across the hall to report to the office next door what had happened and show them the mutilated Bible. They had met this guy, surely they'd know what to do. The doctor across the hall was surprised, but passive. The woman who worked for him wasn't. Neither suggested that I call the police.

I was young and dumb then and simply went back to my office, tidied up and prepared to work that day. The point is, I ate lunch with that woman and a friend of hers two to three times a week. Some of the things that can't be blessed are relationships and alliances with people with dark motives, such as witches, warlocks, wizards, and occultic people.

I've met more than one "pastor" who has dark ties and dark motives. The usual sign is when they look absolutely perfect--, look deeper. Their entire presentation could be whitewashed. One in particular who has what seems to be an immaculate presentation and who has deceived what seems like the entire world, enjoyed great popularity, has a perfect persona especially online. But if you look very closely at his clothing, he wears badges, medals and insignia of Freemasons and Baphomet. He wears this stuff proudly. Saints of God; we cannot be ignorant of trinkets, signs, symbols, jewelry, tokens and tokens of demonic or occultic origin and connection.

There is so much danger to sit under something like that, but if, emulating this "pastor" you pick up the same items, you are initiated and on your way to someplace God is not, and that is no place you'd ever want to be.

What's Inherited

I am talking about trinkets and hand-me-downs, and things that seem neat, cool keepsakes. I'm talking about things that are valuable, or precious, that fall into your possession as well as things you go out to get on your own. Collector's items. You must consider where they've been, whose hands they were in. What kind of person was that and what might they have done to the item, mostly knowingly, but sometimes unknowingly.

I am also talking about things that you go out and buy for yourself. I once had a couple of East Indian batiks in my house that I got from a cultural fair. They were so *different* from what everybody else had. You surely don't think the person who wanted to make a sale asked me if I was a Christian before letting me purchase these things. They weren't Christian, so why would they want to warn me that this would clash with my faith? Surely the person didn't tell me these were idols on the images. No, it was more like, *These are pretty and would look nice on your walls.*

I was so ignorant; those batiks were images of some of the million or so idol *gods* that people from India worship--, Shiva and others. I was no different at that time than the guy with the exotic looking African masks on his wall. The Word says, They know not what they worship. I was guilty of that. Fortunately, after a year or so of calamities, a spiritual someone told me to get those things out of my house. I did. And my life got better. I realize now, in my ignorance that I did not ask God for forgiveness for that idolatry and now I do: Lord forgive me for displaying images of idol *gods* on my wall and for even having their paraphernalia in my house.

Do not bring a detestable thing into your house or you will be set apart for destruction like it. (Deuteronomy 7:26)

I was so proud of the uniqueness and beauty of these items. But were they keepsakes or mistakes? Which is it?

The Bible says that you are not supposed to lose or sell things you have inherited. Remember Naboth would not sell that vineyard to Ahab for that particular reason...

And it came to pass after these things, that Naboth the Jezreelite had a vineyard, which was in Jezreel, hard by the palace of Ahab king of Samaria.

And Ahab spake unto Naboth, saying, Give me thy vineyard, that I may have it for a garden of herbs, because it is near unto my house: and I will give thee for it a better vineyard than it; or, if it seem good to thee, I will give thee the worth of it in money.

And Naboth said to Ahab, The Lord forbid it me, that I should give the inheritance of my fathers unto thee. (1 Kings 2:1)

By Jewish law you're not supposed to let go of something that you have inherited. So where is the balance?

When you inherit a thing and you may suspect it is not good, then you must seek the Lord. By the Holy Spirit you will receive the answer. God will not cause you to inherit something that will curse you, only the devil would do something like that. Discern. Know the difference.

No inheritance... shall pass from one tribe to another. (Numbers 36:7)

The land is Mine; you are but strangers and sojourners with Me (Leviticus 25:23)

(Naboth's Vineyard): Naboth refused to sell his ancestral land because it was part of his family's covenant inheritance.
(1 Kings 21)

Principle: What God gave you as a heritage, you are called to steward, not sell off lightly — especially when it's tied to His covenant or your family's righteous legacy.

`On the other hand: removing the accursed or defiled things is God's way and we see examples of that in the Bible.

Do not bring a detestable thing into your house... it will set you apart for destruction like it. (Deuteronomy 7:26)

Joshua 7 (Achan's Sin): Achan kept things under the ban (cursed items), and it brought destruction.

: Early believers burned their occult possessions — even though they were valuable. (Acts 19:19)

The principle in God is: If an inherited item is tied to sin, idolatry, witchcraft, or unrighteousness, you are not obligated to keep it — and in fact, you are wise to remove it.

What is God-given and righteous, steward it. (Land, legacy, family name, blessings) What is cursed, defiled, or tied to sin, renounce and remove it. (Objects, idols, sinful wealth)

We are called to honor what God gave us, not what the enemy attached to us. Inheritance is a blessing when it comes from God's hand. But if it carries the residue of sin or bondage, it's not an inheritance — it's a burden.

Stewarding inheritance vs. removing the accursed requires discernment. throughout Scripture, God calls His people to walk in wisdom concerning what they receive, hold on to, and pass down. Inheritance is sacred, but not everything passed down is worth keeping.

Stewarding a God-given inheritance is directed by the Word of God, who God gave the people of Israel a physical inheritance: land, heritage, and covenant blessings. These were not to be traded, sold off casually, or discarded.

No inheritance… shall pass from one tribe to another.(Numbers 36:7)

The LORD forbid that I should give you the inheritance of my ancestors! (1 Kings 21:3 (Naboth):

These Scriptures highlight a powerful principle: What God gives, we honor and steward, whether it's land, legacy, ministry, or family heritage. When something is part of a righteous inheritance, it carries purpose, and you are entrusted to protect and multiply it for God's glory.

Removing the accursed thing is needful. On the other hand, Scripture is clear that some things, even if inherited — are cursed, defiled, or dangerous to your spiritual walk.

> There is an accursed thing in your midst... You cannot stand before your enemies until you remove it. (Joshua 7:13:)

> Believers destroyed occult scrolls and items — even though they were costly. (Acts 19:19)

What is cursed, you must cast out — regardless of sentimental or earthly value. Inheritance is a blessing only when it comes from God's hand. If an object is tied to sin, bondage, or idolatry, it's not a treasure — it's a spiritual trap.

Where's the balance? Steward and protect what God has righteously given you. Discern and reject what came attached with sin, manipulation, or occult practices. Let the Holy Spirit guide you in knowing the difference.

For thought:

You are not obligated to protect what God is calling you to purge."

Honor the heritage of righteousness. Reject the residue of bondage.

When something is enchanted or has been used in ritual, or dedicated to idols, leave it. Don't take that into your life or home. Yes, the Blood of Jesus is more powerful than anything, but the 5 second rule does not apply in the spirit. You can't just pick anything up and blow the dirt off of it and say it was only on the ground for a little while. You can't say, it was only in the coven for a little while, and I like it. You can't say that.

Worse, you can't take Uncle So-and-So's stuff that he used in freemasonry and keep it in your house because uncle used it and not you. you can't say uncle used to be a Freemason, but then he stopped, these things he used is just *old stuff*. He's not even a freemason anymore, That paraphernalia is NOT okay.

You can't say this mask is so cool that I must put it in my house; it was only used in a ritual once, or maybe (just maybe) just hoping it was never used for ritual. There is no five-second rule in spiritual matters.

In the Bible, a witch or occultic person might capture and take over a Godly altar and desecrate it. But also, in the Bible God told the people to tear down the evil altars and then replace them with a new ones. He didn't say go wash that off and shine it up and now I will take offerings on it. Would you eat food out of a dirty plate? No; then why do you think God would?

The point is with accursed items in your place they represent an altar. Do you have competing altars in your home? God is not interested in that evil altar and it will be hard to attract Him into your environment. This is especially true of something you wear, or admire often or daily, such as something on your wall whereas God is an afterthought and you may worship or pray only at church.

God is not coming to an evil altar; that is not how you attract God. Nope, tear it down. So in the case of evil trinkets and things, get rid of them, do not try to consecrate them to the Lord. In the case of the possible ritual masks, the person is not an active Christian although he may have been saved years ago. If he was, he is either backslidden or has no knowledge of what a Christian is. Many think just getting saved is all you need to do and then you can do everything else you want to do and still get into Heaven. When I decorated with strange fire—strange batiks, I used to think like that too. I was so wrong.

That's not how it works.

The old Freemason "got saved" but he gave all of his freemasonry *stuff* to a younger relative who then got into Freemasonry. Would a **saved** man give occultic items to another person or would he destroy them? I slashed up the batiks and also burned them so no one else could use them. I didn't give them to a friend whose décor it would match.

You cannot simply say that the person who used it was your cousin and your favorite person or that any of this makes it okay in your case. Spiritual law is spiritual law. God is the only one who can grant exception, not we ourselves because of being sentimental, greedy, foolish, or worse.

Being attracted to accursed items …if you have been foolishly sucked into a competition with another relative to vie for a certain item and you just want to win; will you win?

The Breakup, The Soul Tie

Acts 19:19 shows a perfect example of people voluntarily renouncing and destroying harmful items.

Joshua 7:13 — *"Sanctify the people..."* — cleansing wasn't just personal, it was communal.

Deuteronomy 7:25-26 — "Don't bring abominations into your house, lest you become cursed like it."

2 Kings 23 (Josiah Cleans House) — Josiah purged Israel of pagan items, not just idols but the articles associated with them.

Common keepsakes that can carry hidden influence may include the following:

- Jewelry from toxic relationships
- Artifacts from unknown spiritual origins (statues, masks, beads)

- Gifts given manipulatively (sugar daddy gifts, control gifts)
- Items used in occult, new age, or witchcraft practices
- Letters, photos, or personal effects kept out of guilt, shame, or sentimentality
- This isn't paranoia — it's discernment.
- It's not about throwing away everything, but about asking the Holy Spirit what doesn't belong."

Freedom often comes when you let go of what's been holding you.

Prayer for Breaking Unhealthy Soul Ties

Father, in the Name of Jesus,

I come before You today, ready to be free from every unhealthy, ungodly soul tie — every emotional, spiritual, or physical connection that was never ordained by You, Jehovah.

I renounce every tie, every attachment, and every connection that is not from You.
I break agreement with every soul tie formed through sin, manipulation, lust, control, or ungodly relationships.
I sever every link, every hold, and every spiritual bond that has tied me to people, places, or memories outside of Your will.

By the power in the Blood of Jesus, I declare my freedom.
I command every lingering influence, thought pattern, or desire connected to these soul ties to be uprooted and destroyed.
Holy Spirit, fill every place where these bonds once lived — with Your peace, Your presence, and Your power.

Thank You for deliverance.
Thank You for wholeness.
Thank You for restoring my soul.

In Jesus' Name. Amen.

Declare this: "I am a child of Jehovah God. My life, my home, and everything connected to me is covered by the Blood of Jesus. No curse, no hidden work of the enemy, and no unclean thing can remain. Every ungodly attachment is broken now — and I walk in freedom!"

What's In a Name?

But then there's the name.

What's in a name? Everything. Ask Jabez. Ask Benoni, who was renamed Benjamin very quickly. When you name someone a name that means something negative or evil, you are evoking failure and evil into their life every time you call their name.

When you name your child the name of a previous family member, you are saying that person's lifetime wasn't enough and now this tiny newborn baby has to keep living the life that person who had the name had.

What kind of life was that? Is that what you want for that little baby?

But new parents are often trying to honor their grandparents or other relatives.

Why? Was grandpa a perfect man? Was grandma a saint? They may have been hell raisers with or without your knowledge or back in the day and they not only have iniquity on them that they may have been born with, but they may have contributed to iniquity that is in the bloodline full force. They may have simply stopped their evil ways but never repented. I took down the batiks but failed to repent until the writing of this book, and I had those items decades ago. By ignorance, pride, or oversight a person may stop a behavior or sin, but fail to repent for it.

Naming the child after them only ensures that this is the one who will bear iniquity.

What iniquity? Grandpa was so nice to me.

That's good honey, what did he do in his youth? What problems did he have all of his life, even to death? Was he sickly? Broke? Evil? Sneaky? A cheater?

Then why stick a child with all the *spirits* that Grandpa collected for 80 or 100 years?

Even a Bible name--- I understand in my family there was a great or great-great uncle or somebody named Absalom. My sister thinks that is a really cool name. It is not— even though Absalom may have been one of the finest looking men in the whole Bible, the name Absalom means, *without peace*. Thankfully, no one in my family repeated it.

So even a Bible name – find out what it means and what happened to the person with that name in the Bible. Why would a child have to bear the historical or spiritual consequences of having that name? Knowingly? Especially since you can look it up or read your Bible and just know what kind of life is programmed into that name. Why do you think God told people what to name their children? Because it is important.

Yes, a <u>name</u> can be a keepsake; especially if you name a person a name and they keep it.

That same person, whether you have their name or not--- you got grandpa's watch. You got grandma's pearl necklace--- as a keepsake, you are keeping the life they had going even though they've gone on to glory or wherever they've gone.

The dark kingdom is more avid at recruiting than Christians are at evangelizing, it seems. Even if they have to do it by hook or crook, or by using enchanted or demonic items. Or by causing people to covet accursed items or to bring them into their homes, wear them, or to consume them…they do it *by any means*.

What makes you a mark for witches or makes you attracted to demonic items? It's your blood. You must, therefore repent down your bloodline or you will keep attracting wrong stuff, wrong people, and even wrong pastors.

Did you pray over any of those things you got, inherited, received, bought or were gifted? Or found? Or did you just bring them in the house because they belonged to grandma and grandpa, and this is what we have been taught is LOVE.

Love for what?

Love for who?

Did God say it was okay? Then if you disobeyed the Spirit of God to bring that thing into your house and life, then is it not an *idol* to you now?

Did you anoint them?

How's your life since you brought those things into your possession, into your household?

How are your kids? Kids can be very spiritually sensitive. You bring something just a little bit spiritually off or wrong into that house kids may start having nightmares or acting out. How are your children?

Infertility & Worse Problems

Rachel had Laban's idols. Aside from having infertility problems, and problems in childbirth, even to the point of death we can see how her first child, JOSEPH went through it. Later, we learned how spiritually sensitive Joseph was. This is a strong example of how idols in a home, wrong keepsakes can bring on major setbacks or problems.

Joseph really went through it even at the hands of his own brothers, his own family members. Jacob was in covenant with God big time, but Joseph's mother was an idolater. Or maybe she wasn't – perhaps she was only a thief. She was disrespectful to her own father. But Joseph's grandfather, Laban was an idolater. See how iniquity was stacking up against Joseph from his mother's side, not to mention what Jacob, the supplanter used to be. Joseph had a lot to overcome, and did he not pay and pay and pay, spiritually speaking? What if Joseph had been named Jacob Jr.? What if he had been named Laban to honor his mother's father? Things would probably have been even worse for him.

God named Jesus, Jesus even though God, with more than 99 names could have slapped a Jr. on the end of one of those names and said, there you go. Now I'm proud. I've got a son, and He is named after Me. (People, please.)

Joseph walked upright before the Lord but look at the struggles he had. Yes, Jacob tried to make up the difference and Joseph who was first born of Rachel had firstborn challenges too. Although he was a very wise steward and was Jacob's favorite, but he wasn't the favorite of his ten older brothers.

Rachel had those idols, and the idols probably did _to_ her the very opposite of what she thought the idols would do <u>for</u> her.

So, the "keepsakes" in your home, are they doing anything for you? For your emotions? Possibly. You don't feel guilty for getting rid of something that belonged to someone deceased. For your status in the family? Maybe. You got the *whatever* grandpa left, and your cousin didn't.

Works of the flesh. Get over yourself.

But if the items aren't doing anything for you, what's their purpose in your life? So you can give it to your own child and ruin their life next? So, the idols, evils, demons, and little g *gods* have a flow in your bloodline, and they know which kid is expected to worship them next, and what kid will be tormented?

The Lord God says, Behold, I do a new thing.

Not to mention, Rachel took them from her father who was angry enough to pursue them to get them back, as well as not getting them back, we don't know what may have been spewing out of his mouth; the curses of a parent or authority figure are serious. He could have cursed the person who stole his idols to die the death, not knowing or even caring if it was a relative, even his daughter.

Laban was not saved, but sadly, "saved" people have spoken or done worse.

Rachel does not return Laban's idols in the biblical narrative. She didn't return the keepsakes. Did she throw them away in the desert? The Bible doesn't say, but we must look at the evidence in her life and the lives of others to know more. She is suffering because she has the idols, because she took them and the way she lied and disrespected her father . These are all lessons for us.

Even if Rachel was doing NOTHING with the demons or idols that come along with those idols. The fact that they were in her possession is enough to invite the demons that come along with those items. They caused major problems for Rachel and as we have discussed, her child, Joseph.

In contrast we see Leah didn't have these kinds of problems. Infertility?

Barrenness? No, she popped out 6 boys. And just to prove she could, she also had one daughter, Dinah. However, One day Dinah set out to visit the daughters of the land. Who were those "daughters"? Those were the idols of the land. Dinah got captured and raped and after she was rescued, we heard nothing about her again. We did learn that her brothers did atrocities to the men at Shechem in revenge against the prince of that town who had raped her.

Idols, people. They never lead to good outcomes. Never. The outcomes of the children of Freemasons can be horrendous if they are kept in the dark and don't even know that they are supposed to continue in this cult. Oppression and attacks can result from having items of contact in your possession, no matter who the Freemason was. Even if it is someone that you don't know and never met, but one of these trinkets just ended up in your possession.

Recapping, Rachel steals her father Laban's household idols when she and Jacob flee from him (Genesis 31:19). Laban pursues Jacob to recover his idols, accusing him of theft (Genesis 31:30). Rachel hides the idols in her camel's saddle and deceives her father by claiming she cannot rise because of her menstrual cycle (Genesis 31:34-35).

The narrative does not indicate that Rachel ever returns the idols to Laban, therefore we must believe by the other evidence that she kept them.

Of note here, Benjamin didn't have a jacked up life and that could be because those idols were thrown out of the house or destroyed, possibly returned to Laban when Rachel died. I'm sure Leah or some of those handmaidens went through her stuff after she died and got rid of her things. Rachel still had the idols when Joseph, even though he was a type of Jesus and had good work to do in the Earth, he was affected by the iniquity of his mother, but Benjamin was not because Rachel died in childbirth. And even while she was dying she was cursing that boy, but Jacob intervened quickly and changed the boy's name, thereby changing his life.

Leah and her children went through because of the gods of Leah's father's house, and she may never have known that the idols had been brought to the new place they lived until possibly after Rachel had died (if then).

Teraphim, Terrapin---
DELAYS!

Rachel takes Laban's idols and hides them—well, at least for right then; the story is not told as to what she did with the idols once they got to Canaan, where they were going to live.

In Genesis 31:19, Rachel steals her father Laban's household idols (teraphim) as Jacob and his family flee from Laban. Teraphim are household idols or figurines mentioned in the Bible, often associated with pagan worship practices.

A similar word, but not the same word, terrapin is a type of turtle. And we know that a turtle symbolizes stagnation and delays. When we are speaking of spiritual matters that is what a turtle represents in a dream, for example. When you are dreaming of a turtle, then delay is being programmed into your life. Be sure you pray against this sort of demonic dream programming.

When Laban pursues them, he searches for the idols but does not find them.(Genesis 31:34-35).

Jacob had been at Laban's for 21 years. Laban was trying his best to keep Jacob there to work. How he was doing all this work is a God-thing, a Bible-thing, for sure. Jacob may have been 80 or 85 years old when he married Leah and it was 7 years later before he married Rachel. Wait: Jacob worked the first 7 years for cattle. He worked the next7 for Rachel but got Leah and then he worked another 7 years to marry Rachel. talk about delays, obstacles, switched destinies and attempts at switched destinies. Jacob must have been around 70 years old when he got to Laban's ranch. Jacob was around 70 years old when his mother, Rebecca told him to go to Laban's place to be safe from his twin brother, Esau who wanted to harm him.

Seventy years old--, momma's boy.

You may say Jacob deserved all of this delay because of what he did to Esau....maybe, but there was delay all over that ranch. Laban's ranch—where the idols were.

This family had a lot going on.

Ok, so by the time Jacob married Rachel, she was still of child-bearing age, Bible scholars say possibly in her late teens or early 20's, so how do we not know that she didn't play with those idols and she thought they were toys? She was still in her childhood, after all. Maybe she brought those idols with her because she just liked them? I hate thinking she was that young because Jacob worked 14 years for her, so how old was she when he first saw her?

Saints of God – how many of us would have stayed in the will of God and made it into the Bible if that had been one of us engaged, betrothed, or promised to Jacob? He was already an **octogenarian**, and we were in our teens or early twenties.

As said, she could have played with these idols as dolls -- After all, idol is just doll with an i in front of it. Maybe the letter, *i* in front of a word stands for idol? Does the letter, *i* in front of a thing stand for *idol*? How many people are attached to their iPhone? Is the iPhone an idol? It's always in our hands. We are always looking at it; isn't that worship? We carry it around with us. We think it's going to do something for us. If we leave home without it, we go back and get it. Is an iPhone an *idol*? People steal them, isn't this how idols are treated?

Your Father's House

Anyway…what did she do with them? We do not know, but <u>that</u> she stole is bad enough, but *what* she stole was even worse. These idols most likely were a point of contact for those idols of her father's house. That is the same for any item, jewelry, trinket, token, art piece, anything inherited, found or gifted to you. Consider the source, always.

Points of contact? Yes: Laban's idols: We pray against the idols of our father's house all the time. If you too, pray against the idols of your father's house, yet you have Grandpa's watch, daddy's ring, grandma's whatever – that may mean that whatever idols they were serving for the 70, 80 or 100 years they lived, plus the idols from their own father's house – could be different or additional idols, or it could be the same ones only deeper embedded into the foundation of that bloodline. Those idols are expecting whomever owns this piece now to do the same. When you don't worship or do as the previous owner then the idols riot. They go into an uproar.

When that item is one of their items, one of their symbols, or has been dedicated by them or to them, it gives them an open door and a right to come into your life and live with you.

You're not worshipping it because you now profess Christ? Then the attacks will begin. This item is an open door for them to come in and expect worship.

Ask yourself, what has happened to your life since you got that thing you inherited or that thing that fell into your hands? That thing you find on vacation or at a cultural festival that is not your culture. Or that thing that you went to a secondhand store or a pawn shop and purchased?

Graven image means a figure that represents an idol *god*, itself. But there is a *god* for everything: you like gold? There is a *god* for that. You like leather? There is a *god* for that. You like silver, diamonds, amethyst… you name it, there is a *god* for that.

This must be why we are warned about adornments in the New Testament, and we don't worry so much about what is on the outside, but more of what is on the inside because idol gods attach themselves to things they know humans will like and covet. They do this to garner worship even from unsuspecting people.

Your Daddy's Suit: Garments

Specifically, since this book is about your deliverance: Could something or some things that are in your house be the cause for a delay in your deliverance? Even things that you have forgotten that you have? Things you have put away in a safe place for some day in the future, or for some day when you want to gift or burden your child with that thing???

How's your marriage? Should your daughter wear your wedding gown if your marriage has been horrible or is not good at all? It's not just what the dress looks like as to why a daughter may reject her mother's or grandmother's wedding dress. This thing is spiritual. So, you want her to honor grandmother? Does grandmother deserve that kind of honor? Should she honor grandma at any cost? Aa a sacrifice to her own life, success, or happiness? Does grandmother need that honor?

If Grandma is demanding she wear the dress—watch it. The man who honors himself; it is no honor at all.

Garments: Careful of what you receive and how you give things away. Be sure you pray very well over things you both give and receive, whether you wear them on your body or not, but especially if you do. Everything that you own, wear, even things that have been around you not only have your DNA on them, if they've touched your physical person, but they also have your spiritual signature on them. In the spirit, anything that is yours or was yours can be matched back up to you or associated/identified as yours by anyone who is spiritual and who wants to know.

Garments and other possessions. Especially wallets and purses, and handbags. Careful of things that represent your money. You got dad's favorite wallet, but he was *broke* all the time?

Get rid of that thing.

Don't you wipe your computer or cell phone – you pull the SIM card or chip out of it before you sell it, give it away or dispose of it? It's kind of like that: your spiritual signature is on your things, your clothing for example. Else, why would touching the hem of Jesus' garment have drawn virtue out of Him? Why would Paul's handkerchiefs have healed? (Acts 19:12) Why would Peter's shadow have healed? (acts 5:15-16) Their essence was all over things that pertained to them and things that touched them. and so is yours – good or bad.

And the kingdom of darkness knows this and also works to put demonic charges on things and stuff and items to effect evil outcomes in the lives of their victims and intended victims—people that they want bad things to happen to—to harm, or hurt, or to initiate.

Dear Christians, we should not be so passive, we should be blessing stuff in our possession so if and when it gets in the hands of folks--, maybe it could heal them, save them, or at least stop them from doing evil.

Achan: Joshua and the whole camp had a problem with Achan who saw goodly Babylonish garments and things and brought them into the camp, so much a problem that the presence of these things troubled the whole camp.

When I saw among the spoils a goodly Babylonish garment, and two hundred shekels of silver, and a wedge of gold of fifty shekels weight, then I coveted them, and took them; and, behold, they *are* hid in the earth in the midst of my tent, and the silver under it."(Joshua 7:21)

Achan took these things as keepsakes, he coveted them and took them. If a few things can trouble an entire encampment of people, how much can a wrong thing in your house trouble you, and interfere with your success, your life, your progress, your marriage, your fertility, your ministry? How much can it interfere with your deliverance? Especially if you are not aware that it is a problem and have not even prayed over it or tried to pray over it? Or even tried to bless it, anoint it, or consecrate it – it's just there. It's just there because you found it or somebody gave it to you and you thought it looked cool, or cute, or different. Or worse, you were guilt-tripped into keeping it or you thought it was valuable?

But it sits there in your house, looking pretty, or it is in a drawer somewhere "safe." and you've forgotten all about it.

Souvenirs

The things you brought home from exotic vacations that you have come to know are known places for witchcraft, for example—what about those things you brought home from those witchcraft places? Where are they? Have they affected your life since you put them in your house either in a drawer or on display? Since you hung them on your ears, around your neck or wrist? Or in a closet?

I went to such a place to shop. At the steps of the place, my spirit man did not like or want to go in there. I said to my then husband, I'm not going in there. He wanted to know why? I said, "Witchcraft, there is too much witchcraft going on in there."

What makes a shop such as a souvenir or antique shop "safe" or "unsafe" spiritually?

Most antiques — furniture, dishes, jewelry — carry nothing harmful. They're just old.

Objects with History: Some items, especially from certain cultures, wars, occult practices, or secret societies, may have a spiritual "history" attached to them.

Ritual Objects, Idols, or Occult Tools: These are the risky ones. Things used in ceremonies, witchcraft, cults, or dedicated to false gods may carry spiritual baggage.

A thing could have a spiritual charge on it because the person who made it is a whole witch and they have prayed to their *gods* for the item to sell. It is enchanted so when you see it, Oh, you can't take your eyes off it. You love it. If you pass it by you think about it all day until you go back to get it. Be spiritually suspicious here and pray about it.

Personal Effects Tied to Sin or Trauma: Like letters, jewelry from toxic relationships, or items associated with violence or crime could be spiritually dangerous.

As mentioned: in Joshua 7 (Achan's Sin) — Objects forbidden or devoted to destruction brought trouble. And in Deuteronomy 7:26 — "Do not bring a detestable thing into your house..." Also, in Acts 19:19 — People burned occult objects after coming to Christ.

The safest approach for Christians is to:

- Pray before buying — literally ask God to give you discernment.

- If you feel a check in your spirit, walk away.

- Cleanse the item in prayer if you acquire it and bring it home.

- Be cautious with items that have unknown origins, especially spiritual artifacts, symbols, or ritual tools.

Not every antique is a spiritual threat. But some antiques come with unseen baggage — and it's better to be discerning than sorry.

An island souvenir market may have simple cultural Crafts and also have those that are mixed with spiritual practices Many handcrafted items may be sold there — carvings, jewelry, masks — are inspired by local folklore, African spiritual traditions, or Obeah form of folk magic). Even if sold as "souvenirs," some items may be replicas of ritual tools, spirit symbols, or objects tied to ancestral worship.

Obeah & folk practices are still embedded in many cultures. Obeah is still practiced in parts of certain islands that have a real occult system.

With my discernment turned off, I purchased a few small tapestries to give as souvenirs when I returned from an island vacation. That's been 10 or more years – I have no idea where those things are. I cannot find them anywhere. I pray to the Lord that they have long been discarded and destroyed. Thank God, He didn't let me gift those things to anyone.

Some artisans or sellers may craft or sell items they *knowingly* dedicate to spiritual purposes — for protection, power, wealth, or manipulation. You "rich Americans" who think these things are so unique and cute, could be actual targets. If these items are used for evil exchange, for example, you might see a downturn in your favor and finances if you bring these things into your life.

Not just on exotic islands, but any marketplace can be as a Spiritual Portal. Open-air markets, especially those selling folk crafts, can sometimes operate under a mix of spiritual influences — not all godly.

Think of it like Acts 16 — Paul met the slave girl with the spirit of divination *in the marketplace.*

Markets in Biblical times were often spiritual battlegrounds and I'm sure that was to teach us.

Discernment is real and it is really necessary. If you felt uneasy — that's the Holy Spirit, full stop. It doesn't mean everything there was evil, but the atmosphere carried mixed spiritual traffic. It doesn't mean that you should be so guarded that you don't enjoy your vacation. It doesn't mean that you should support local artisans. But if the Holy Spirit is telling you something, you don't even have to explain it naturally — your spirit didn't settle, and that's enough.

At that first island marketplace that I mentioned, my then-husband laughed and laughed at me and insisted that I go in.

I couldn't.

DON'T QUENCH THE HOLY SPIRIT. If there is a check in your spirit, do not override it....don't go to places, don't buy things, don't get things, don't receive things if the Holy Spirit is telling you, NO or Don't. That means on vacation as well as domestically. It doesn't matter who it is from – grandma, grandpa, your favorite person---

That keepsake could be a whole mistake; it could make all the difference in your life, and in your deliverance. today and in the future.

It could make a huge difference in the lives of your children.

Domestically, if we look at the high-value or rare masonic items then we know that those things do move from house to house. This list is not so you know what to go look for to make money, it is to advise you to use caution in case you see any of these things.

- Vintage Masonic Aprons — Hand-embroidered or leather aprons from the 1800s or early 1900s can fetch serious money.

- Antique Masonic Swords — Especially Knights Templar swords engraved with names, dates, or lodge insignia.

- Old Ritual Books — Early editions, hand-inscribed, or secret code versions from rare jurisdictions.

- Masonic Pocket Watches — Custom watches engraved with symbols — big among collectors.

- Jewels of Office (from Defunct Lodges) — Official lodge jewels from now-closed lodges are rare.

- 19th-Century Masonic Medals or Coins — Some minted only once for grand events.

- Masonic Bibles (Early Editions) — Often family heirlooms with genealogy notes.

- Rare Lodge Pins (From International Lodges) — Especially pre-World War pins from European lodges.

The collection of a longtime member might include:

- A travel case of regalia
- Several aprons
- Dozens of pins or medals
- One or two swords (if in higher bodies like Knights Templar)
- Ritual manuals or officer's guides
- Commemorative items from conventions

Which of the above items are occultic or accursed? **ALL OF THEM.**

Some ex-members have auctioned their items — especially if they held office or were active internationally — and some of those lots have sold for hundreds to thousands of dollars.

In the natural, the marketplace is a place of trade — money, goods, services. But in the spirit, marketplaces have always been more than that. Discern your environment and especially the marketplace spiritually.

There were more than a few marketplace encounters in the Bible.

- **Acts 16:16** — Paul met a slave girl with a spirit of divination *on the way to the place of prayer*. The enemy often operates where people gather.
- **Matthew 21:12-13** — Jesus overturned tables in the temple marketplace — a place meant for worship but corrupted by greed and exploitation.
- **Acts 19:24-27** — Demetrius the silversmith stirred up a riot over Paul's preaching because it was bad for his idol-making business. The marketplace is where commerce, culture, and spiritual influences collide.

- **Where money, which represents life and is also used for exchange or sacrifice is that place is considered an altar**.

All of this matters to believers because Spiritual atmospheres don't change just because you're a tourist. Some markets, especially in regions with a history of witchcraft, idol worship, or spiritualism, still operate under influences unseen. Items for sale may carry more than cultural value. They may carry spiritual significance.

Remember, if you feel unsettled or spiritually "pressed" upon entering. If you sense heaviness, confusion, or even anger for no reason. You notice a lot of items tied to occult symbols, idolatry, or dark folklore, pay attention.

If you hear conversations or sales pitches that seem manipulative or spiritually off, be aware! I saw a travel show where the host was so happy to go to a shop in Brazil that had carvings of many of their local *gods*. Spiritually clueless, thinking that stuff only affected old people, (I guess). She happily thought nothing of it except the items were cool and she wanted to know the history of some things before she purchased them.

Pray before you shop and also while you are shopping. Pray when you take out your money or credit card. (Money exchanges is another book entirely, but who you hand money to is also a deeply spiritual matter.) Ask the Holy Spirit for wisdom. Don't override a spiritual check. If you feel not to go in or buy, trust that. Bless and cover yourself. Declare your spiritual covering in Jesus' Name before entering unfamiliar spaces. Remember: You're not fearful — you're discerning.

Saints of God: the marketplace has always been a battleground for the soul — for what you buy, what you take home, and sometimes, what you open your heart to. Stay sharp. Stay prayed up. Stay led. Stay covered.

Rachel Died

Even though you may feel obligated to hold on to that thing that grandpa left you --- check with God. What does the Spirit say. You may even have been duped, fighting with another sibling because you want it over them. If in the marketplace you saw someone else wanted a thing so you quickly bought it before they could – just because you could. Maybe you were at an auction, and you definitely wanted to win. Maybe what you got is valuable, but is it expedient for you to have? Is it spiritually correct for you to have it.

Maybe you're the one who is supposed to get it – according to the plans of the devil...he wanted to wreck something in your life.

LORD, don't let me fight for anything that I am not supposed to get, have, or keep, in the Name of Jesus.

Leah had a husband who didn't even love her and she had 6 boys for him. In the Bible, and even now, having a boy is everything, even though it is the husband who determines the gender of the child, not the mother. Leah's delay--, yes, she also had delays was that her husband did not love her and she kept expecting that son after son, one day he would.

Rachel got the husband who loved her but she had fertility issues and died in childbirth. **BECAUSE SHE HAD THE IDOLS;** she had the items—the keepsakes that ultimately were mistakes.

Consider carefully where you are getting things that you bring home and into your life – especially OLD things. Old doesn't make them better. New doesn't make them better or worse. Check with God --, getting permission from God, in the first place and dedicate those things to God before bringing them home.

I'm not telling you not to go antiquing if that is what you like to do, but check in with God first and whenever you find something you want--, things you want to bring home ask the Lord first.

Consider seriously:

- Items that belong to a dead person:
- Items that belonged to a person who died suddenly or traumatically, questionably.
- Mysterious deaths are often witchcraft-related or occultic. For example, a person who dies on their birthday is usually a result of witchcraft. That is why you should fast and pray on your birthday versus partying since it can be a very vulnerable time, spiritually.
- Items that belonged to an occultic person or witch – whether you know it or not. Whether they knew it or not – if you suspect, or even know, don't accept those things…

Real life: A woman ended up with her father's watch; he was deceased. It wasn't instant, but her life began to stagnate from that day. More than once, the Holy Spirit reminded her to get rid of that old, broken timepiece, but she got distracted and forgot it. The Spirit reminded her several more times over many years, and finally she got rid of it. She wasn't trying to quench or ignore the Holy Spirit, it's just that the cares of this world distracted her – often.

Her natural father had also died in a suspicious way--- not only that, but a -- watch or clock that doesn't work, doesn't run—can stagnate your progress in life. It can stagnate a breakthrough, it can stagnate a deliverance. You have a watch or clock that doesn't run- are you a clock or watchmaker? Are you repairing it? Then why is it at your house? If it just needs a battery – put a battery in it. Keep fresh batteries in it or get rid of it. Old things that don't work—fix them or get rid of them.

Dead plants. Dead things – get them out of your house. Especially if you have noticed that you are suffering stagnation.

A woman gave a beautiful ruby ring that she had inherited from her grandmother to another person to clean it for her. The woman who owned the ring disappeared, nobody can find her. She was a professional woman who worked in a bank, and we know bank workers are well vetted, but many years later, she is still not to be found. The woman who gave the ring lost her husband in a terrible accident before the ring was left to be cleaned. The woman who kept the ring for her, though she never wore it, had trouble staying married and is single to this day. It's As though the original owner of the ring did a cut and run. It's as though she is hiding because she doesn't want that thing back. Even her former best friend has no idea where she is.

The woman who harbored that keepsake for all these years, eventually got rid of it and her life began to get better from that very day. Before that she had been in a marriage and after the marriage, I had dated two fellows seriously, but each one just one day said, *Bye*. No real reason. It was usually, the *I'm not happy* line. This woman is lovely, sweet, doesn't nag, and has her own money. They just leave. This is very anti-marriage and suspicious. The husband actually told her that if they didn't break up, he felt he would die. This all screams *spirit spouse.*

If you think about it spiritually, what happened in the house of the woman whose grandmother gave her that ring, could have transferred to the person who now has it. Husband gone? First hers, then the next person who had the ring? Perhaps a *spirit spouse* came with that ring. The owner of that ring lost her husband in a freak accident; did the *spirit spouse* get rid of the first woman's real husband? They can be dangerous and violent, after all. Who can say, except the Lord, through the Holy Spirit. So, stay prayed up and discern.

Of course you want to know about the freak accident. One night the owner of the ruby ring's husband was working on the floor or subfloor of the living room repairing a rotted board and the floor gave way and he fell into the basement of their house. He didn't die; she rushed him to the hospital. At the hospital the man, who was a drunk was so belligerent and uncooperative that he was rolled over into a corner to sober up and then they'd be ready to help him. By morning he was dead. At the hospital. In the ER, brought in alive, but dead by morning.

So, you have or get an item from someone or someplace, even though it's valuable, don't make it a keepsake, that is a mistake.

People want you to let them store things at your place? You'd better find out exactly what is what, and what is in those boxes or crates. Aside from unknowingly harboring illegal things, there may be spiritually illegal things that will affect your house, family, business, or ministry.

But if it is an item that you are looking right at, ask, What is the history of the item? The real history, not the made-up sales pitch if you are purchasing the item. Ladies, when you get a diamond ring from someone it means you are getting into an alliance with them. That is the same with items, objects, signatures, trades. Exchanges all confirm contracts and make covenants and alliances. You've got to know where or from whom the things you get are coming – what is their spiritual history? What is their story?

Can't Get Rid of Some Things (Easily)

There are some things you get that are next to impossible to get rid of...things that become a part of you, such as another person's DNA... Selah. Let me be clear without being too graphic; women when you receive DNA from a man while in a sexual act, since you are receiving that into yourself, it becomes a part of you.

What is the history and the outcome of the person who owned the item that you're looking at or about to acquire? Is your intention to be permanently and spiritually connected to them? Is their intention the same? They said so. Do you believe them? And you want that? God okayed it? Then, good.

Idols or no – stolen things…will curse and not bless. If something is hot, that is stolen and it's worth $500 and the cost is $5, don't buy it. It is accursed. It costs $5 in the natural, but in the spirit, it could cost you everything. Do not bring that thing into your house. Accursed things belong to devils, demons, and little g *gods*. When they see that item it is like a bat signal for them to stop over at your place and they can stay as long as that item is there --, because it is theirs. And you, a human? They claim you as theirs as well. Don't have it in your possession or bring it to your house.

Keepsakes- can be the whole reason there is delay and stagnation in your life. You should have been promoted by now. You should have been pregnant by now. You should have had a successful business of your own by now. It is stagnation that is holding you up Also, if you keep stagnant things in your house such as stagnant water that is spiritually contributing to the problem.

Wash your dishes. Clean your house. Get rid of stuff that you are not using and know you will not be using again. Go through those boxes of things in the garage, attic, or basement that you plan to get to someday. Make that someday today. If you can't do all the boxes at once, do one box a week, or every couple of weeks. Just start; the Lord will help you. Get rid of those things correctly though.

Yes, you have prayed and fasted, and cried out to God day and night and praised and worshipped and built an altar to the Lord by giving sacrifices. And yes, you're expecting the King of kings to show up. And God wants to show up—and He does, but you're cozy up in your house with another in there – with an idol? Let's say it's only one.

- Your keepsake is an idol.
- Or a dedicated item?
- And item used in ritual.
- An accursed thing?

You think it's art, but it's been used in ritual, and you have it on your wall because you think it's cool? Or its on your finger because you think it is so unique? OR SO VALUABLE? Or, you're showing off—you got it, and Cousin Bob didn't. or you're too emotional and sentimental, this was granddad's ring, so you wear it around your neck every day on a gold chain.

Really?

While you are holding on to accursed things, it makes it possible for the devil to rob you. And it keeps God away from you.

Return to Me

All that the Father giveth me shall come to
me; and him that cometh to me I will in no
wise cast out. (John 6:37)

But God says: Come back to Me –
return unto Me and I will return unto you. we
are praying for God to give us the blessings
He has for us, and to give us back the things
the devil stole from us. And God may very
well be saying something like this the whole
time, **All the things the devil took; I have
them; I kept them for you. But you've got
to return to Me before you get them.**

God may be saying, **I was only
waiting for you to come back to Me.**

When you realized that the things you
are supposed to have, you don't have them.
And you realized that things you were not
supposed to have, keep, or use--, but you

have them --, that's when you will fully realize that those keepsakes that were mistakes. So, you finally got rid of those things, and repented. Then that is when you also self-delivered, or you at least participated in your own deliverance if someone else was praying for your deliverance. Being delivered, now you can walk out of captivity. The captivity that the devils, demons, and little g *gods* installed around your life, or placed you into. If they can stagnate you, that will slow you down slowly enough to be captured.

But you are now fully delivered, and you have walked out of that keepsake, idolatry trap. Amen!

You may be thinking that you haven't turned your back on God – maybe you didn't – on purpose. But when you were drawn away by another lust, when something caught your attention, caught your eye, or you began coveting things and stuff, or harboring the enemy's stuff at your house that was at least an initiation, but it was a turning away from God.

IF RACHEL WAS SERVING GOD, WHEN SHE TOOK THOSE IDOLS FROM LABAN, SHE TURNED AWAY FROM Jehovah GOD RIGHT THEN. WHEN SHE DIDN'T GIVE THEM BACK TO LABAN, SHE REALLY DOUBLED DOWN on turning away from God. BECAUSE: There is a curse in dishonoring father and mother – so Rachel was stacking up iniquity, *big time* by idolatry, stolen items, harboring those items, lying to and dishonoring her father.

We know about Rachel's suffering and outcomes.

When Did You First Notice?

When did things change in your life? Go back and ask yourself, when did they begin to change?

Job said there was a time when his steps were like butter ---

When his candle shined upon my head, *and when* by his light I walked *through* darkness; As I was in the days of my youth, when the secret of God *was* upon my tabernacle; When the Almighty *was* yet with me, *when* my children *were* about me; When I washed my steps with butter, and the rock poured me out rivers of oil; When I went out to the gate through the city, *when* I prepared my seat in the street! The young men saw me, and hid themselves: and the aged arose, *and* stood up. The princes refrained talking, and laid *their* hand on their mouth. (Job 29:3-9)

Job was respected; Job had favor. Job was honored. But things changed. When did you last notice favor or peace or abundance? Or respect? What changed? Ask yourself seriously what changed? And when did it change?

A lady came to me with serious dry mouth. The usual question is, *what changed?* Additionally, Are you taking a new medication? Usually that is the answer. A person with a new skin irritation or itch – should ask themselves, what changed? Your soap or shower gel? Your laundry detergent or softener? *What changed?*

Or for the person who notices something physical has changed, look spiritual to see if something in the spirit has changed. Even after noticing when spiritual things change, **what** changed? *Who* changed? Did you start dating or associating with someone new? Did someone give you a gift that you accepted and put in your house, or around your neck or wrist? Or your body? What changed? Who changed? Who changed around you?

Look even deeper – did your dreams change at that time? At what time? When you met a new person? When you started a new alliance with someone that you already knew? When you brought a certain new thing into your house? What changed?

And the Word of God says: RETURN UNTO ME AND I WILL RETURN UNTO YOU…

The Book of Malachi talks about tithes and offerings? Okay, the Word of God is true and I will not dispute it. But God needs you to return to God as yourself. Because God came down in the cool of the day to walk and talk with Adam. But one day He couldn't find Adam. And He said, ADAM WHERE ARE YOU?

I believe God was looking for Adam by his glory, but Adam's glory was gone because he had been disobedient and sinned. When you follow idols and accept idols you lose your glory because they came to take your glory, to steal it. When you sin you lose your glory. God is looking for you.

WHERE IS YOUR GLORY?

RETURN UNTO ME AS YOURSELF, as the one I created and formed so I will see and recognize you. RETURN TO ME AS YOURSELF, NOT WITH ANY DEVILS, DEMONS, OR IDOLS ON BOARD. **Just you**.

RETURN UNTO ME DELIVERED and whole. FULLY DELIVERED AND IN YOUR GLORY SO I CAN walk and talk with you, in the cool of the day. And I can FURTHER GLORIFY YOU, I CAN FURTHER ANOINT YOU, I CAN FURTHER BLESS YOU, SAYS THE LORD.

RETURN UNTO ME AND I WILL RETURN UNTO YOU.

This is how you return to GOD. you must return as yourself—. Just you.

Get rid of the saddle that is on your camel, get off your high horse. Get rid of your idols and unknown or *known* demonic and occultic keepsakes, trinkets, tokens, and et cetera. Then return to your Father, God.

HOW DO I KNOW THIS? The Holy Spirit told me. Not only that, God is particular --- how do I know that?

Joshua the high priest's garment had to be changed to get into the presence of God. His outfit. His garment. Pay attention because details are important. We are no longer under the Law; we are under Grace. Our Father God is a God of Grace, but you don't show up to God in kinda way you want -- all tacky, although you can come as you are right now to be saved.

Those of us who are saved and are supposed to know better, do better, be better. When will our conversion be fully accomplished? When will we come into the nature of the perfect man, becoming more and more like Christ?

God has the right to expect us to grow up spiritually, to be fully converted.

Jesus came to save sin-sick man... to save us from eternal damnation, from sickness, death, poverty--- so we are supposed to be converted from that from

114

what we were before Jesus – before Jesus came, before we met Jesus, before we accepted Jesus -- to now we *become--,* to look more like Jesus more each day.

Jesus didn't have idols. Jesus didn't have treasures in Earth. We are warned about that in the Word. It says, Do not store up for yourselves treasures in earth... Matthew 6:19. This is a way to keep us from wrong keepsakes, to help keep us from mistakes.

Everything God says is to protect us.

PRAYERS

Lord, have Mercy on me a sinner. If I am none of Yours, Lord, give me a Godly sorrow for my sins and a repentant heart, and make me one of Yours, in the Name of Jesus.

Holy Spirit, fall on these prayers, in the Name of Jesus. Amen.

Blood of Jesus flush out of my system everything ever given to me, deposited with me, or in me that was intended to stay with me to mark territory, or given as a *keepsake* that I now know was a mistake, in the Name of Jesus.

Lord, break me free from every inherited *keepsake* whether physical or natural or spiritual, that is not from You, of You, or like You, in the Name of Jesus.

Lord, I consecrate all my gain to You, so that You will be in everything I have, get, hold, keep, use, or wear, in the Name of Jesus.

Lord, I bless everything I give away, may these things be used for good and never for evil against me or anyone who receives them, or anyone else, in the Name of Jesus.

Father, everything I give, I remove my essence, I remove my DNA, I remove my spiritual stamp off of it, in the name of Jesus – make it spiritually neutral, in the Name of Jesus.

Lord, remove from me and my possession, my house and my car, my place of business every idol, in the Name of Jesus.

Father, by Your Spirit point me to anything at all in my house that I have acquired, reccived, gotten, inherited, bought, or that I've been gifted that I have in my possession that I should no longer have so that I may remove it, in the Name of Jesus.

Lord, show me how to dispose of things that I should no longer have in my possession or house, or workplace, in the Name of Jesus.

Lord, if I am in a wrong garment, change my garment so I may enter into Your presence, in the Name of Jesus.

Lord, in the Name of Jesus show me anything in this house that my children may have brought in that should not be here. Anything accursed, anything that is a mistake, anything that is from the dark kingdom, so that I may remove it, in the Name of Jesus.

Lord let me speak to my children and teach them at all times so that they know better, in the Name of Jesus.

I bind and render every *spirit of stagnation* powerless against me, in the Name of Jesus.

I remove every *idol* from my environment, my body, my life, my spirit, soul, in the Name of Jesus. I declare that Jesus is LORD. Amen.

Father, I break the *spirit of barrenness, infertility* and all *unfruitfulness* in me and against me, in the Name of Jesus.

Spirit of Death, I render you powerless against me, my life, my success, my business, marriage, and destiny because Christ has redeemed me from the Curse of the Law, in the Name of Jesus.

Lord, forgive me if I have stolen anything from anyone at any time. Show me if anything demonic, occultic, witchy, stolen, evil or any item that represents an evil alliance in anyway with the dark kingdom, is anywhere in my possession, workplace or house, in the Name of Jesus.

I break the *spirit of hoarding* off of me so I am not tempted to keep unnecessary things, in the Name of Jesus.

I bind up a *covetous spirit* so I do not covet things, in the Name of Jesus.

Lord, forgive me, if I have ever lied to a parent or anyone in authority especially to keep an idol or any other stolen item, in the Name of Jesus. Lord, have Mercy on me.

Blood of Jesus wash me clean from every sin or theft, wash me clean of all idolatry, lying, in the Name of Jesus.

I renounce and denounce idolatry in the Name of Jesus. I remove all idols and keepsakes, mistakes from my life and I renounce any initiation because of those items, in the Name of Jesus.

I break and cancel all worship to any evil idol because of any dark and evil items in my possession, in the Name of Jesus.

I reject every evil item and idol, in the Name of Jesus.

I reject every evil name, and I do not accept the life of anyone who does not exemplify the life of Christ and support the life that You intended that I would live here on this Earth.

Lord, let me love what You love and hate what You hate, in the Name of Jesus.

I break all communion with the dark kingdom, in the Name of Jesus.

I break all alliances, agreements, covenants, contracts and communion with idols, devils, demons, and little g *gods*, in the Name of Jesus.

I break all relationships, conversations and communion with evil and evil entities, in the Name of Jesus.

Lord, restore me to Communion with you, communion with the Holy Spirit and with Your Word and all things that pertain to You, and to the Kingdom of Light, in the Name of Jesus.

Father, reverse all damage done to me, my life, my marriage, my spouse, my family, my ministry, my destiny, my business and finances because of dedicated or accursed items formerly in my possession, in the Name of Jesus.

Lord, restore to me what has been taken from me, in my disobedience, rebellion or ignorance, Blood of Jesus speak for me, plead for me, in the Name of Jesus.

Lord, restore my life, redeem the time, restore the years, repair my life, , in the Name of Jesus.

Renew me, renew in me a right spirit and remove every evil spirit from my mind, spirit, body, and soul, in the Name of Jesus.

Father, make me clean and in my right garment so that i return to You and Lord return to me, in the Name of Jesus. return me to right relationship with You and restore my Glory all to and for the Praise of Your Glory and for the sake of Your purpose in my life, in the Name of Jesus.

Thank You, Lord for hearing and answering prayers.

I bless and adore You, Lord. Thank You, Lord. Thank You, Jesus.

I seal these words, decrees, declarations and prayers across every dimension, age, era, epoch, timeline, past, present, and future, to infinity. I seal them with the Blood of Jesus and the Holy Spirit of Promise, in the Name of Jesus.

Any retaliation against the speaker, listener, or anyone praying or will ever pray these prayers, decrees and declarations in the future – Lord let that retaliation be rendered null and void and return with Fire on the head of the perpetrator, without Mercy and to infinity, in the Name of Jesus.

Amen. *Thank You, Lord. Hallelujah!*

I *am* the LORD: that *is* my name: and my glory will I not give to another, neither my praise to graven images. (Isaiah 42:8)

Dear Reader

Thank you for acquiring and reading this book. Thank you for supporting this ministry.

May the Lord make you keenly aware of any keepsakes that are mistakes in your possession so that you can be rid of them and then return to the Lord your God and He will return to you. Amen.

Shalom,

Dr. Marlene Miles

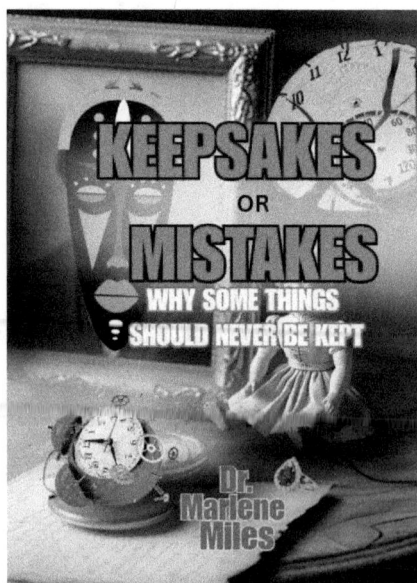

Prayerbooks by this author

While most books by this author have prayer points either throughout the book or at the end, there are some books that are only prayers. You just open up the book and pray.

Prayers Against Barrenness: *For Success in Business and Life*

Fruit of the Womb: *Prayers Against Barrenness*

Beauty Curses, *Warfare Prayers Against* https://a.co/d/5Xlc20M

Courts of Marriage: Prayers for Marriage in the Courts of Heaven *(prayerbook)* https://a.co/d/cNAdgAq

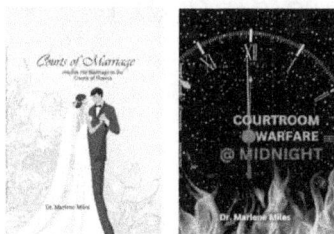

Courtroom Warfare @ Midnight *(prayerbook)* https://a.co/d/5fc7Qdp

Demonic Cobwebs *(prayerbook)*
https://a.co/d/fp9Oa2H

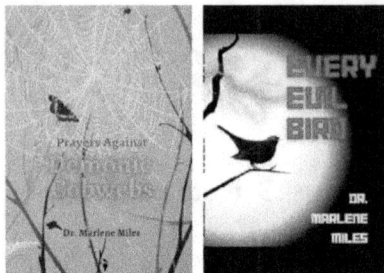

Every Evil Bird https://a.co/d/hF1kh1O

Gates of Thanksgiving

I AM NOT YOUR TARGET: *Warfare Against Haters & the Powers They Employ*

Spirits of Death, Hell & the Grave, Pass Over Me and My House

Throne of Grace: Courtroom Prayer

Warfare Prayer Against Poverty
https://a.co/d/bZ611Yu

Other books by this author

AK: The Adventures of the Agape Kid

Already Married in the Spirit: *Why You May Not Be Married in the Natural*

AMONG SOME THIEVES
https://a.co/d/dkYT4ZV

Ancestral Powers

Anti-Marriage, *The Spirit of*

Backstabbers https://a.co/d/gi8iBxf

Barrenness, *Prayers Against*
https://a.co/d/feUltIs

Battlefield of Marriage, *The*

Beware of the Dog: Prayers Against Dogs in the Dream.

Bless Your Food: *Let the Dining Table be Undefiled*

Blindsided: *Has the Old Man Bewitched You?* https://a.co/d/5O2fLLR

Break Free from Collective Captivity

Broken Spirits & Dry Bones

By Means of a Whorish Father

Casting Down Imaginations

Churchzilla, The Wanna-Be, Supposed-to-be Bride of Christ

Demonic Cobwebs (prayerbook)

Demonic Time Bombs

Demons Hate Questions

Devil Loves Trauma, *The*

Devil Weapons: Unforgiveness, Bitterness,...

The Devourers: Thieves of Darkness 2

Do Not Swear by the Moon

Don't Refuse Me, Lord (4 book series)

https://a.co/d/idP34LG

Dream Defilement

The Emptiers: *Thieves of Darkness, 1*
https://a.co/d/5I4n5mc

Evil Touch

Failed Assignment

Fantasy Spirit Spouse
https://a.co/d/hW7oYbX

FAT Demons (The): *Breaking Demonic Curses* https://a.co/d/4kP8wV1

The Fold (5-book series)

- The Fold (Book 1)
- Name Your Seed (Book 2)
- The Poor Attitudes of Money (3)
- Do Not Orphan Your Seed (4)
- For the Sake of the Gospel (5)
- My Sowing Journal

Gang Ups: Touch Not God's Anointed

Getting Rid of Evil Spiritual Food

https://a.co/d/i2L3WYQ

got HEALING? Verses for Life

got LOVE? Verses for Life

got HOPE? Verses for Life

got money? https://a.co/d/g2av41N

Here Come the Horns: *Skilled to Destroy*
https://a.co/d/cZiNnkP

Hidden Sins: Hidden Iniquity

https://a.co/d/4Mth0wa

How to Dental Assist

How to Dental Assist2: Be Productive, Not Wasteful

How to STOP Being a Blind Witch or Warlock

I AM NOT YOUR TARGET: *Warfare Against Haters and the Powers they Employ*

I Take It Back

Keepsakes or Mistakes:

Legacy

Let Me Have A Dollar's Worth
https://a.co/d/h8F8XgE

Level the Playing Field

Living for the NOW of God

Lose My Location
https://a.co/d/crD6mV9

Love Breaks Your Heart

Made Perfect In Love

Mammon https://a.co/d/29yhMG7

Man Safari, *The*

Marriage Ed. Rules of Engagement &
Marriage

Made Perfect in Love

Money Hunters: Beware of Those

Money on the Altar https://a.co/d/4EqJ2Nr

Mulberry Tree, *The*
https://a.co/d/9nR9rRb

Motherboard (The) ~ *Soul Prosperity Series*

Name Your Seed

Occupy: *Until I Return*
https://a.co/d/bZ7ztUy

Plantation Souls

Players Gonna Play

Portals: Shut the Front Door: Prayers to Close Evil Portals.

Power Money: Nine Times the Tithe
https://a.co/d/gRt41gy

The Power to Get Wealth
https://a.co/d/e4ub4Ov

Powers Above

The Robe, Part 1, The Lessons of Joseph

The Robe, Part II, The Lessons of Joseph

Seasons of Grief

Seasons of Waiting

Seasons of War

Second Marriage, Third~~, *Any Marriage*

https://a.co/d/6m6GN4N

Seducing Spirits: Idolatry & Whoredoms

https://a.co/d/4Jq4WEs

Shut the Front Door: *Prayers to Close Portals* https://a.co/d/cH4TWJj

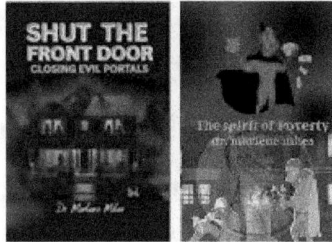

Sift You Like Wheat

Six Men Short: What Has Happened to all the Men?

SLAVE

Soul Prosperity soul prosperity series 3

https://a.co/d/5p8YvCN

Souls Captivity soul prosperity series 2

The Spirit of Anti-Marriage

The Spirit of Poverty
https://a.co/d/abV2o2e

Spiritual Thieves https://a.co/d/eqPPz33

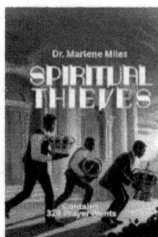

StarStruck~ Triangular Power series.

SUNBLOCK~ Triangular Power series.

The Swallowers: *Thieves of Darkness*, 3

Take It Back

This Is NOT That: How to Keep Demons from Coming at You

Time Is of the Essence

Too Many Wives: *Why You Have Lady Problems*

Tormenting Spirits
https://a.co/d/dAogEJf

Toxic Souls

Triangular Power *(series)*

- Powers Above
- SUNBLOCK
- Do Not Swear by the Moon
- STARSTRUCK

Unbreak My Heart: *Don't Let Me Die*

Uncontested Doom

Unguarded Hours, *The*

Unseen Life, *The* (forthcoming)

Upgrade: How to Get Out of Survival Mode

- Toxic Souls (Book 2 of series)
- Legacy (Book 3 of series)

The Wasters: *Thieves of Darkness,* Bk 2
https://a.co/d/bUvI9Jo

What Have You to Declare? What Do You Have With You from Where You've Been?

When I Was A Child, *I Prayed As a Child*

When the Devourer is Rebuked

https://a.co/d/1HVv8oq

The Wilderness Romance *(series)* This series is about conducting a Godly relationship and marriage with someone who is a Wilderness person. It is about how to recognize it and navigate through it. These books are about how not to get caught up in such.

- *The Social Wilderness*
- *The Sexual Wilderness*
- *The Spiritual Wilderness*

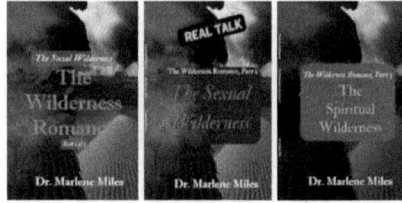

Other Series

The Fold (a series on Godly finances)
https://a.co/d/4hz3unj

Soul Prosperity Series https://a.co/d/bz2M42q

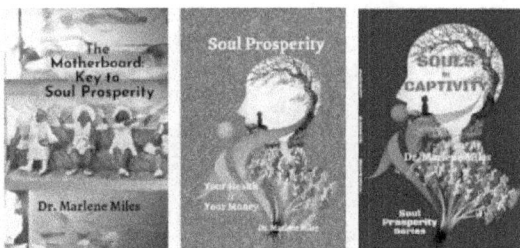

Spirit Spouse books

https://a.co/d/9VehDSo

https://a.co/d/97sKOwm

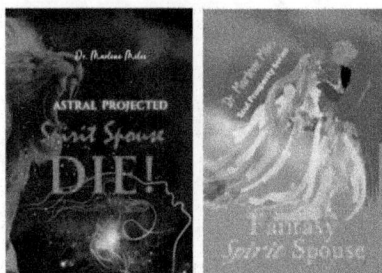

Battlefield of Marriage, The

https://a.co/d/eUDzizO

Players Gonna Play

https://a.co/d/2hzGw3N

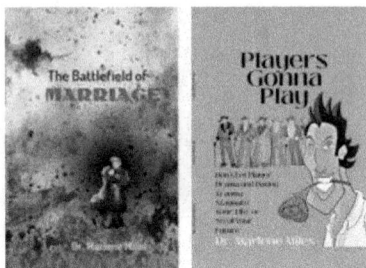

Sent Spirit Spouse (can someone send you a spirit spouse? This book is not yet released.)

Matters of the Heart

Made Perfect in Love
https://a.co/d/70MQW3O

Love Breaks Your Heart
https://a.co/d/4KvuQLZ

Unbreak My Heart
https://a.co/d/84ceZ6M

Broken Spirits & Dry Bones
https://a.co/d/e6iedNP

Thieves of Darkness series

The Emptiers https://a.co/d/heio0dO

The Wasters https://a.co/d/5TG1iNQ

The Swallowers https://a.co/d/1jWhM6G

The Devourers: Why We Can't Have Nice Things https://a.co/d/87Tejbf

Spiritual Thieves

Triangular Powers https://a.co/d/aUCjAWC

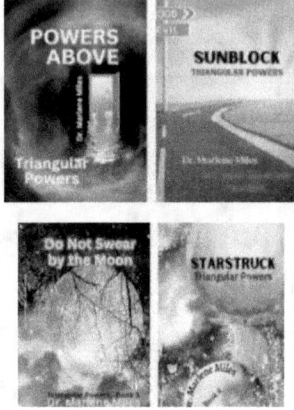

Upgrade (series) *How to Get Out of Survival Mode* https://a.co/d/aTERhXO